A Book of Drawings

by Betsy Streeter

ISBN: 978-0-9777264-6-2

First Printed: September 2015

For Rob, Jen and Sean, and my parents.

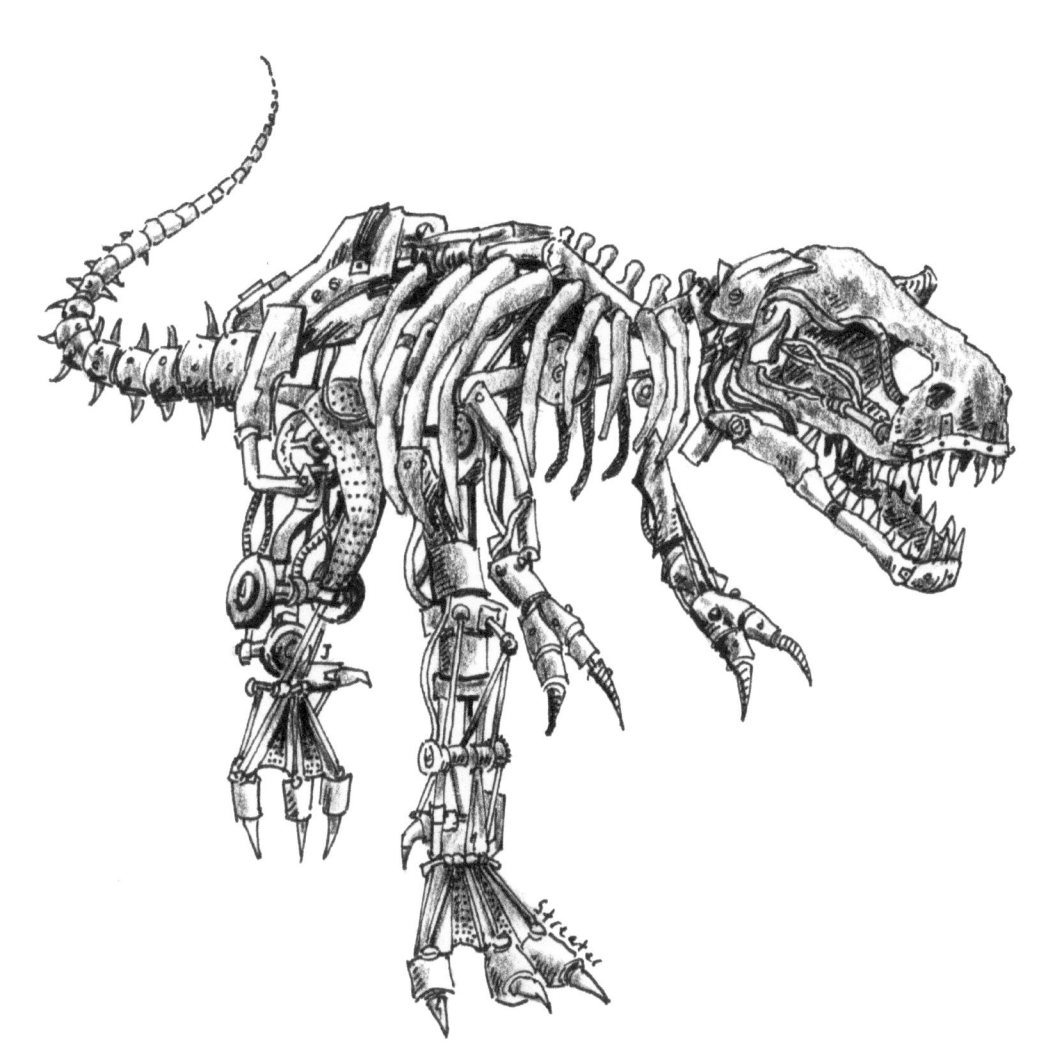

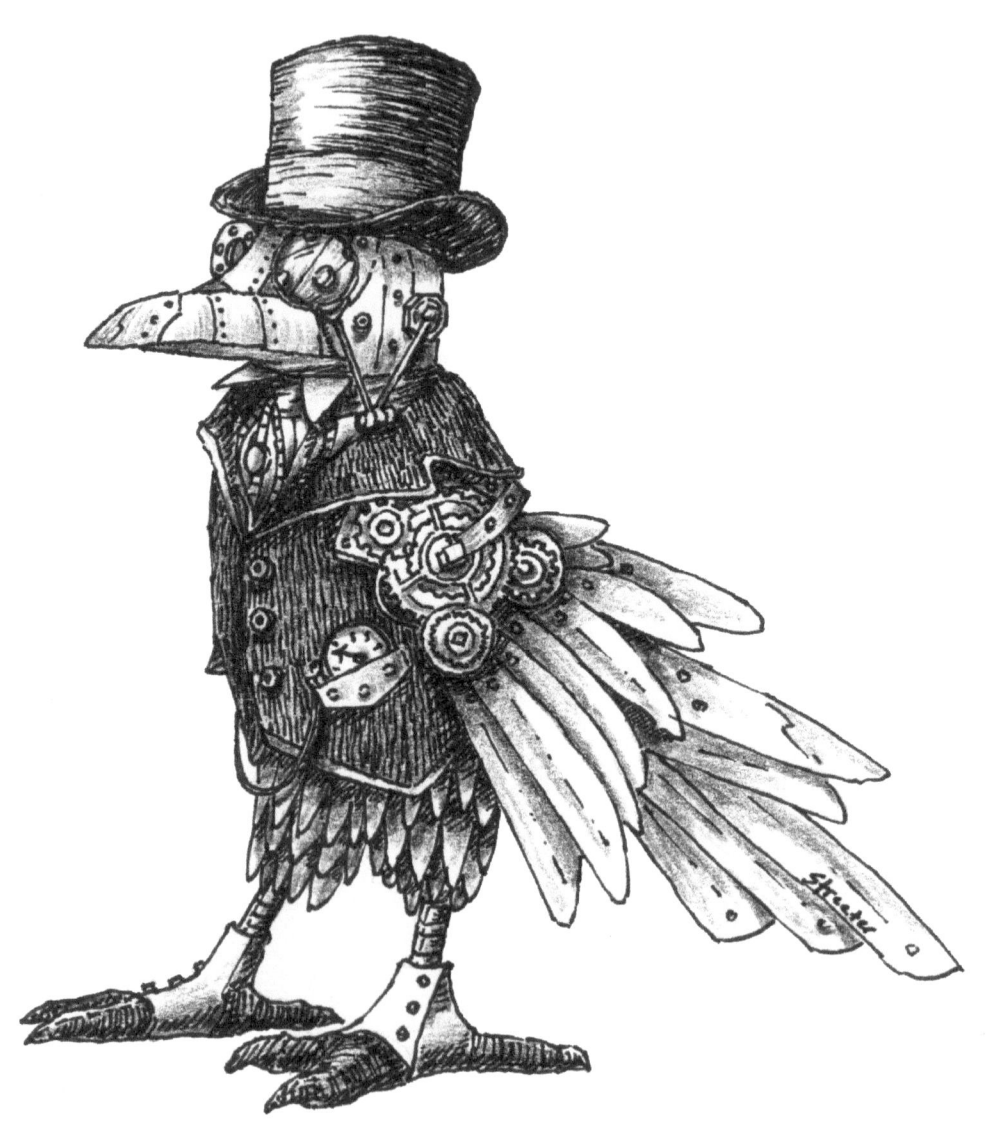

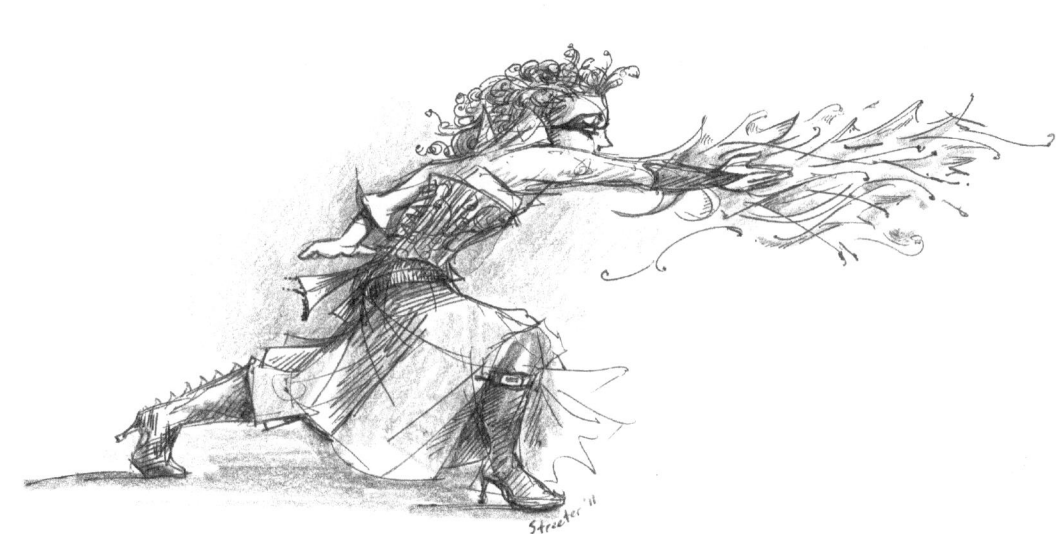

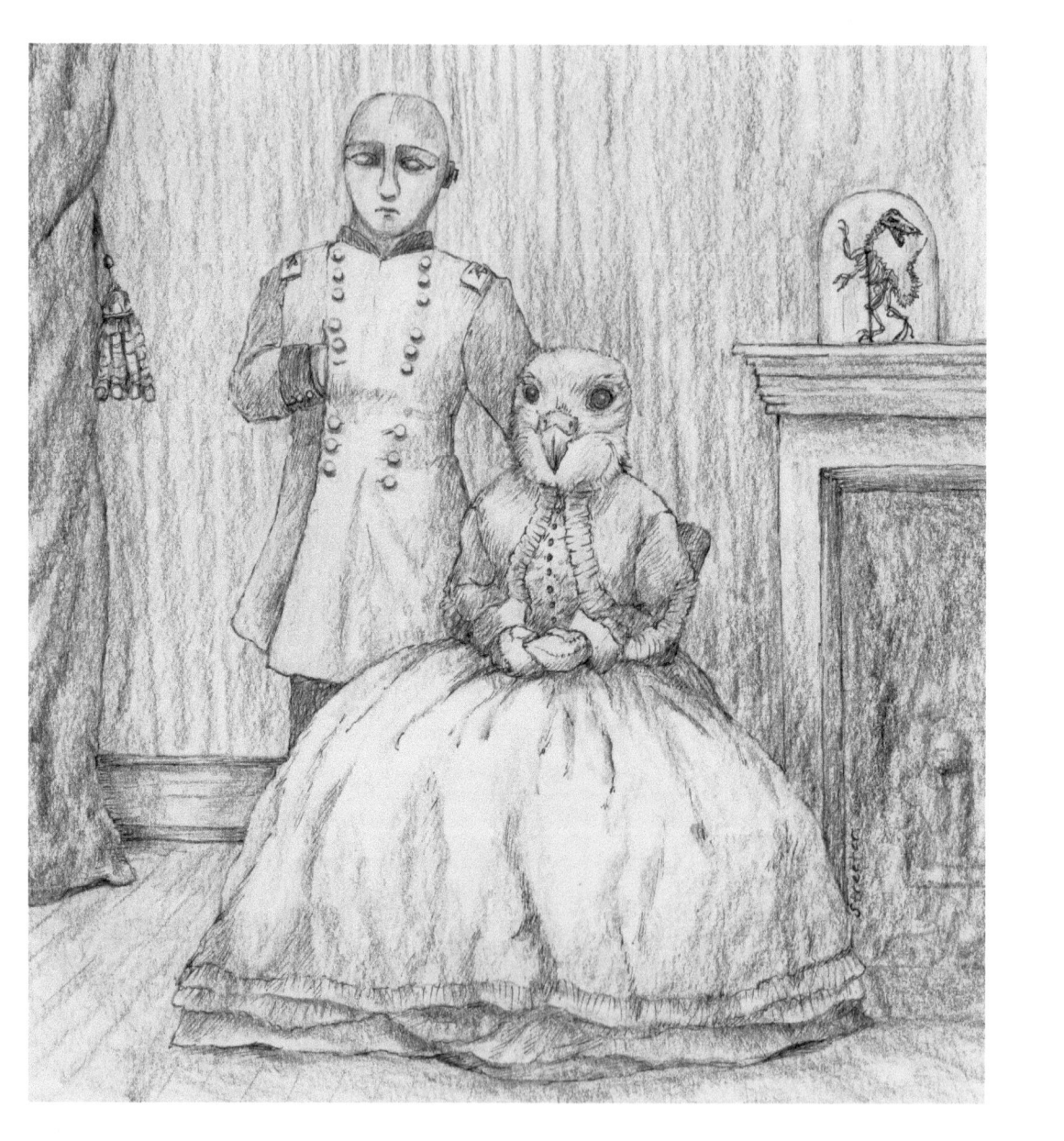

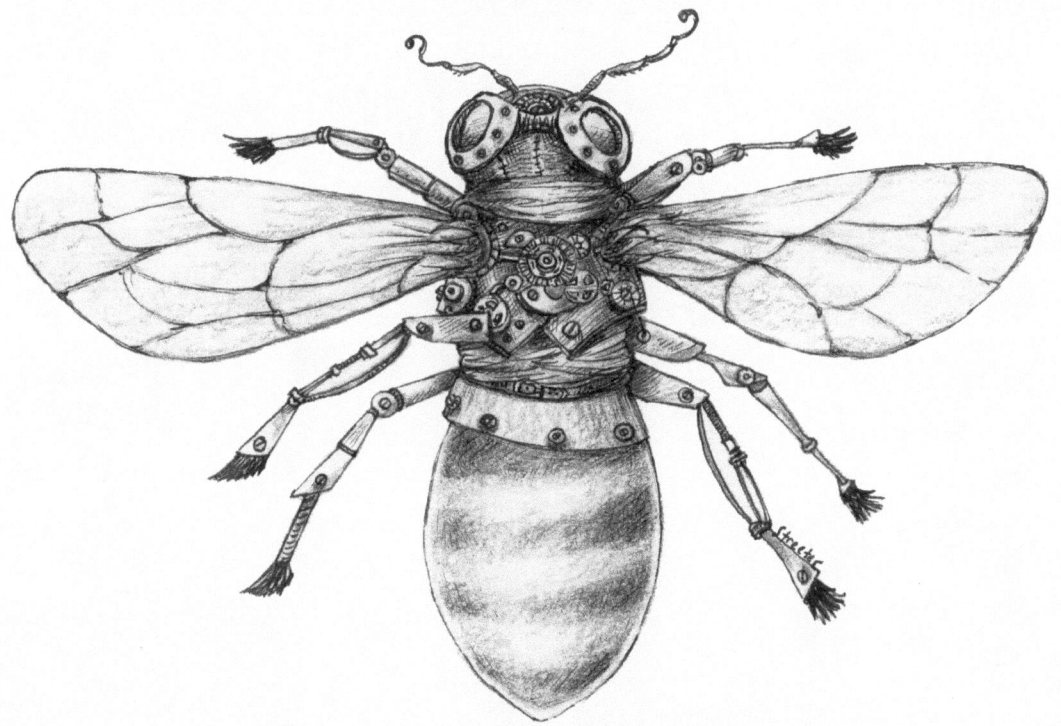

SAVE The BEES

" THE COSMOS IS FULL BEYOND MEASURE OF ELEGANT TRUTHS
~ OF EXQUISITE INTERRELATIONSHIPS
~ OF THE AWESOME MACHINERY OF NATURE "
~ CARL SAGAN

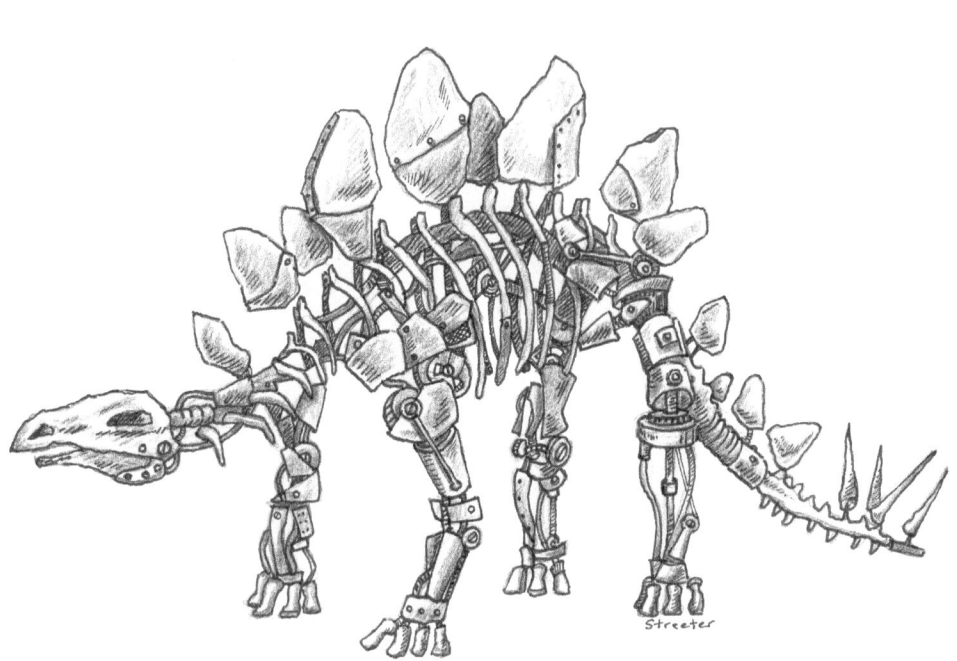

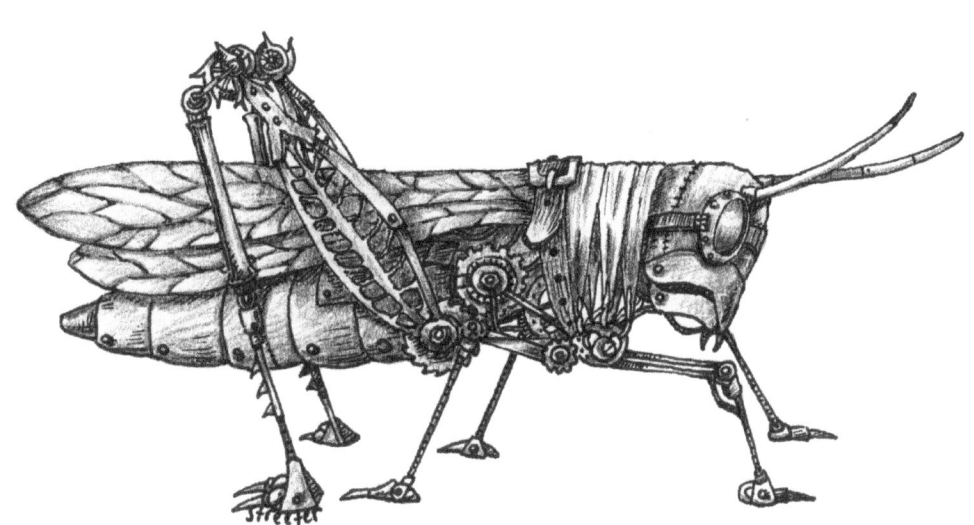

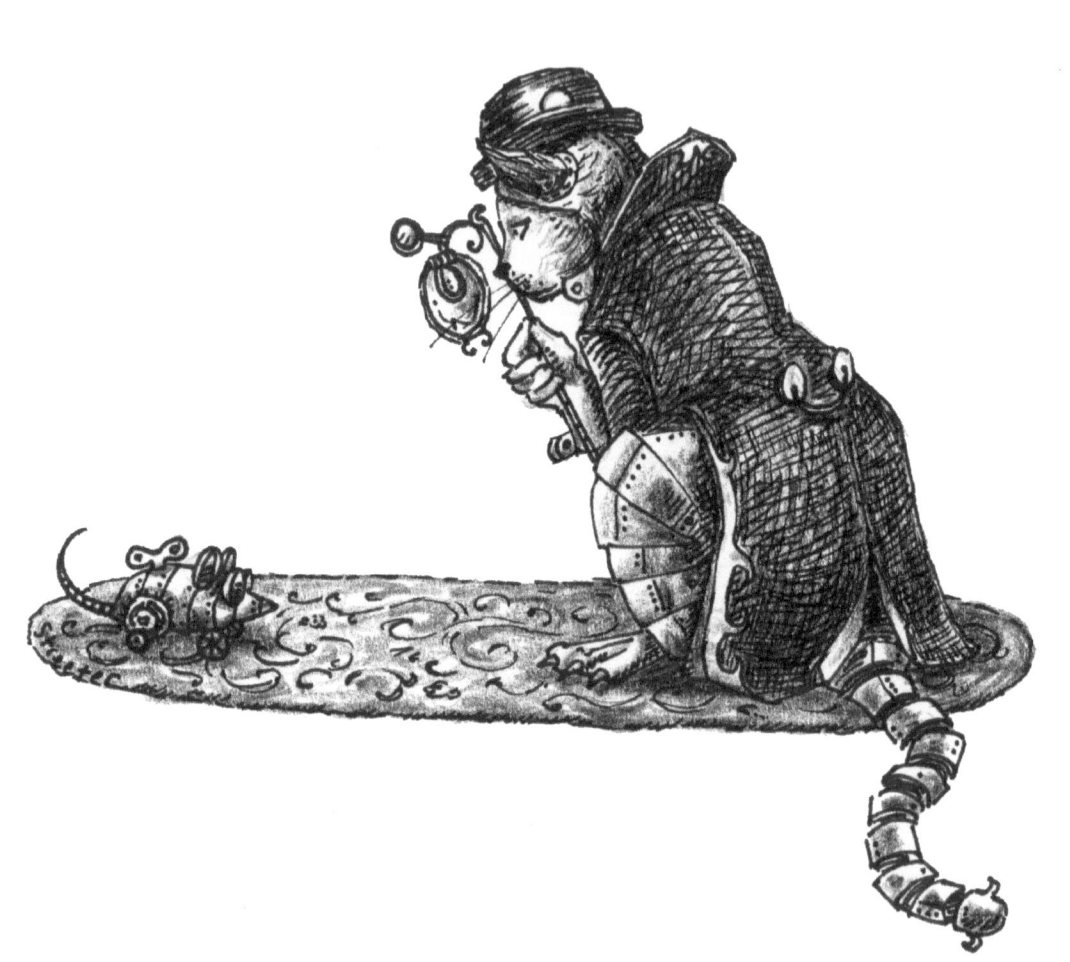

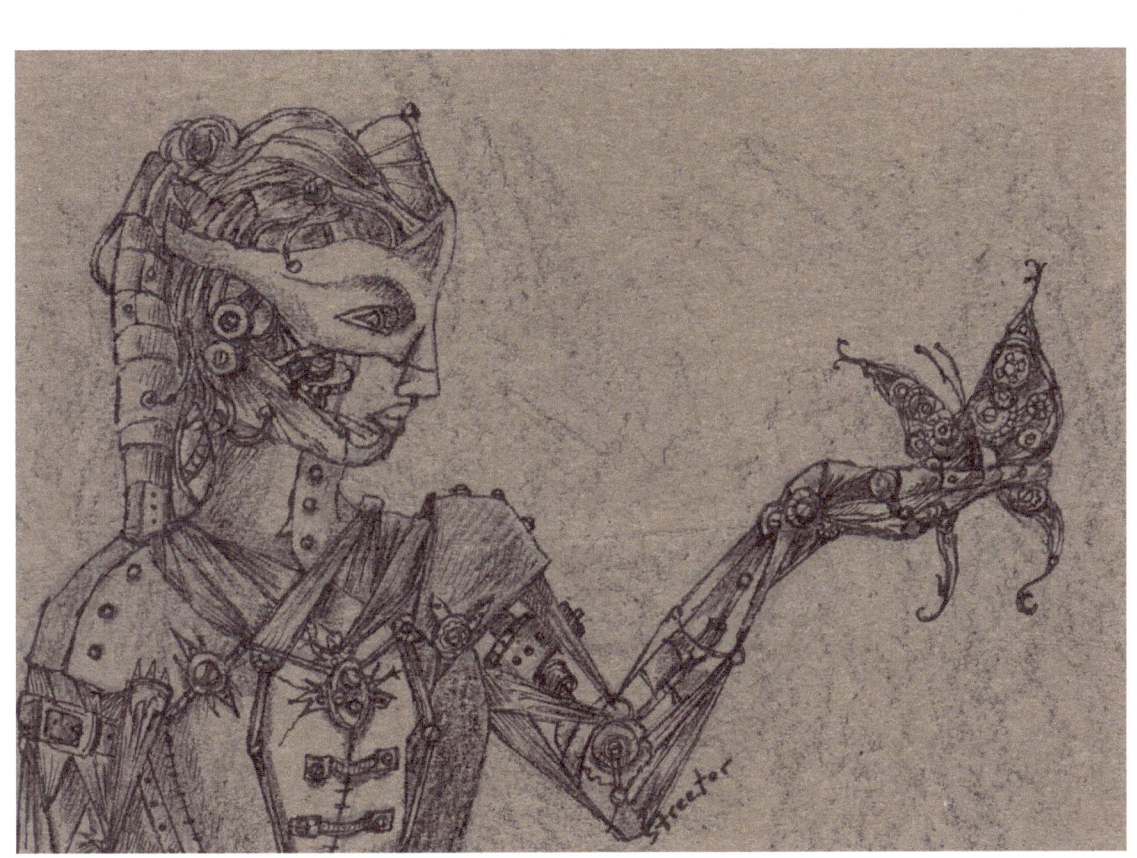

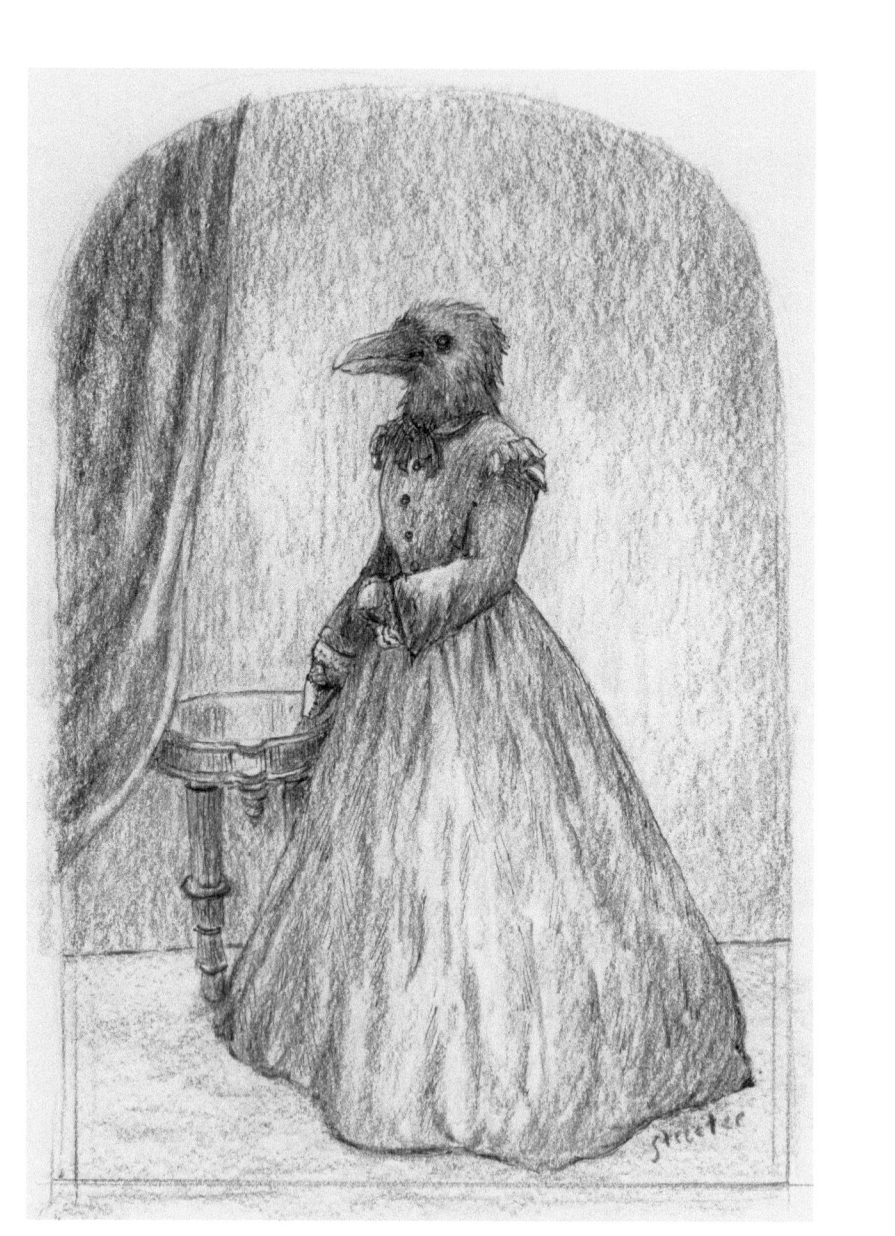

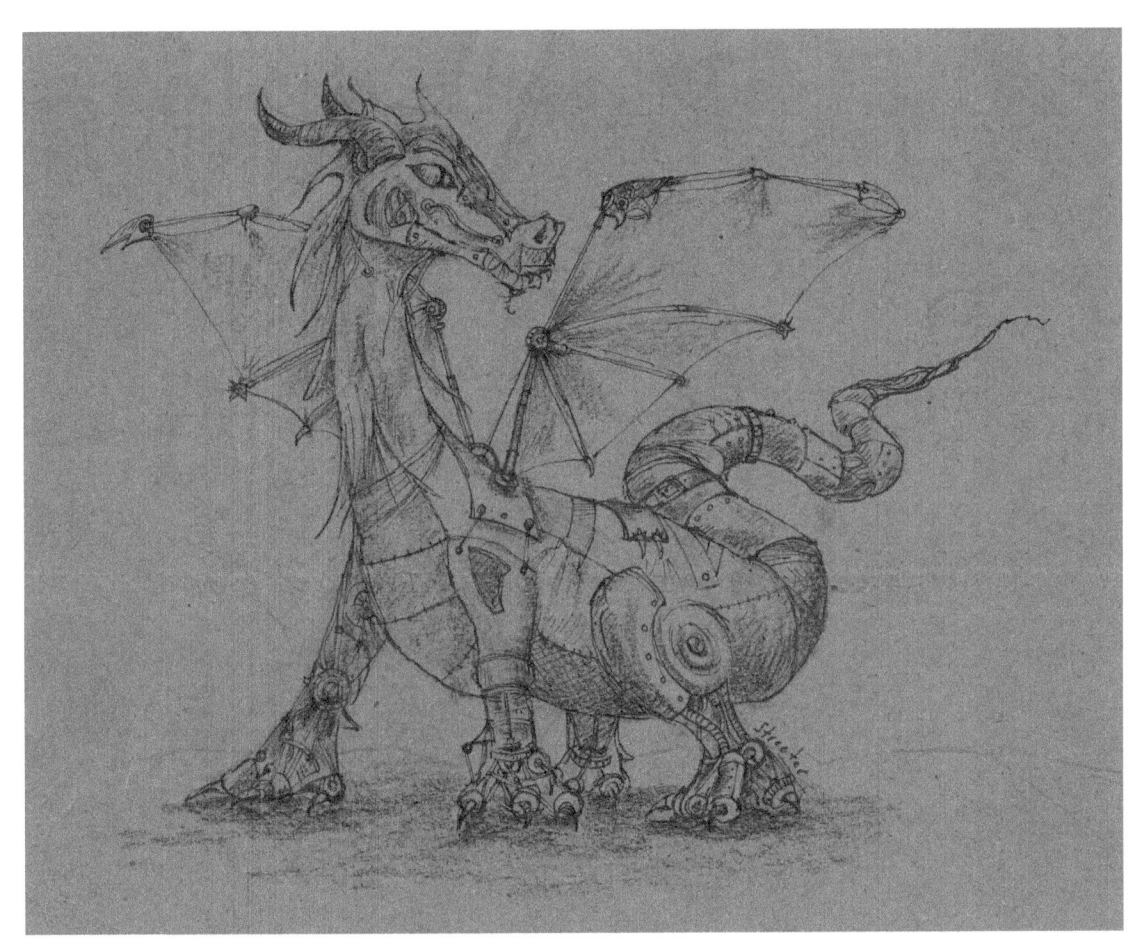

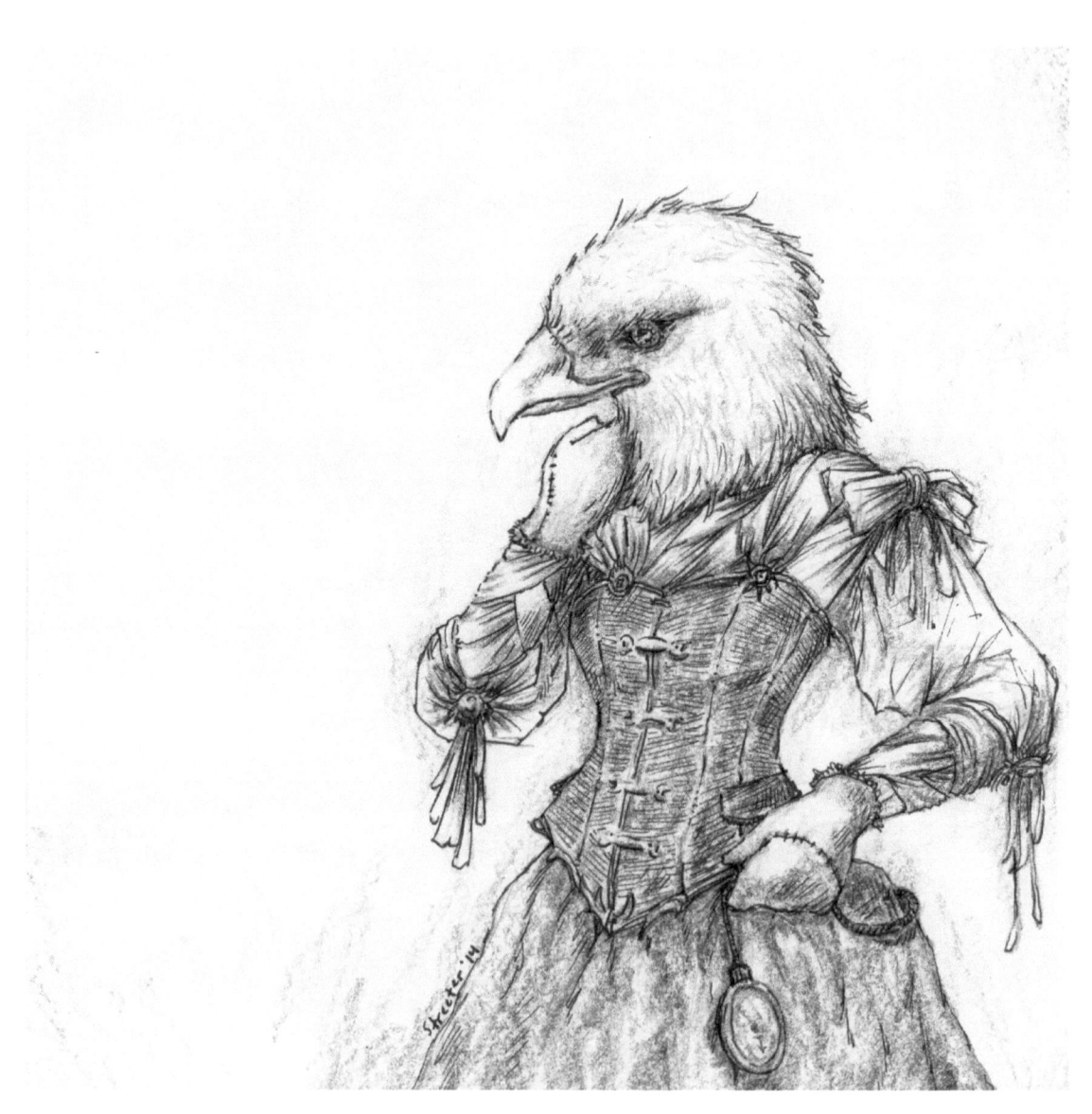

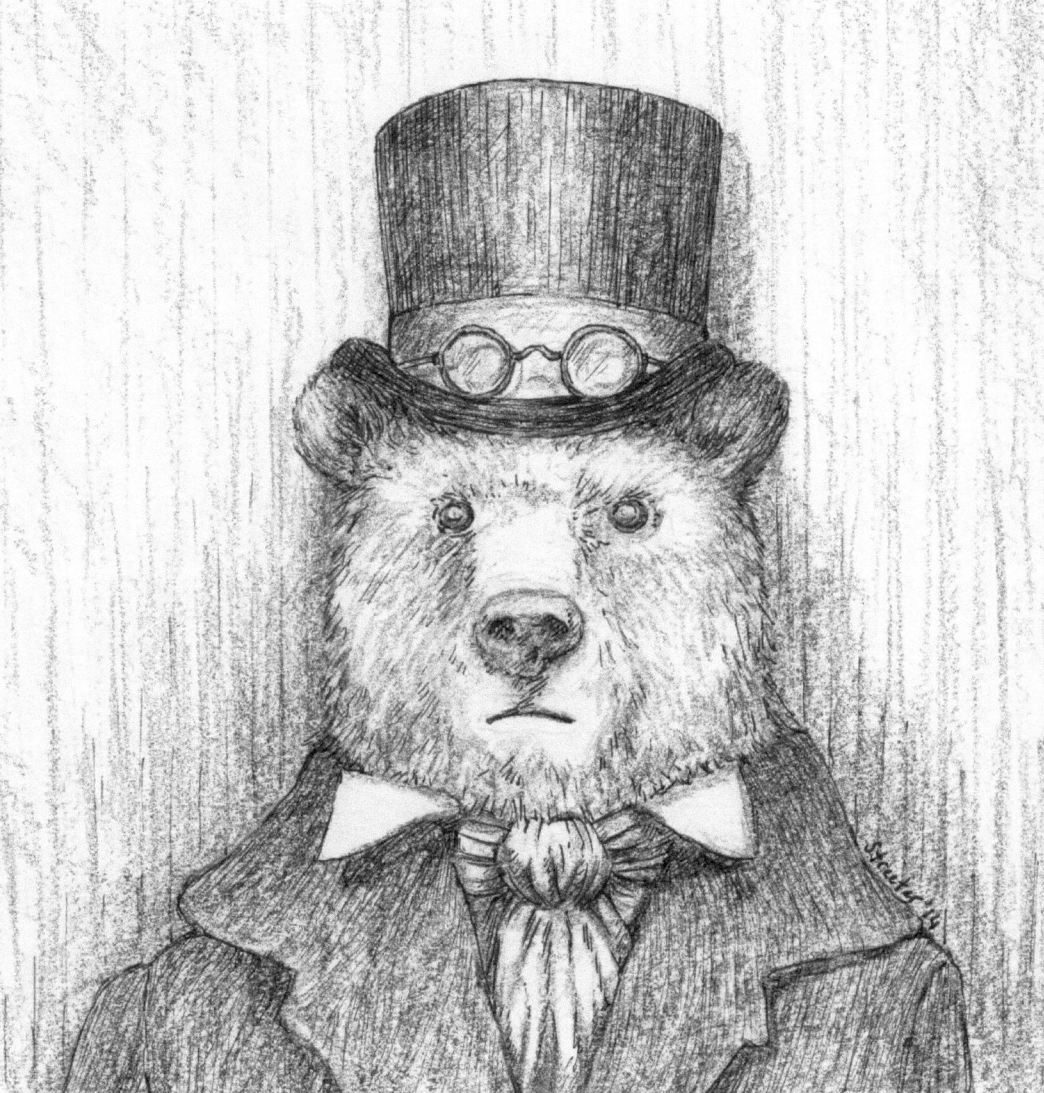

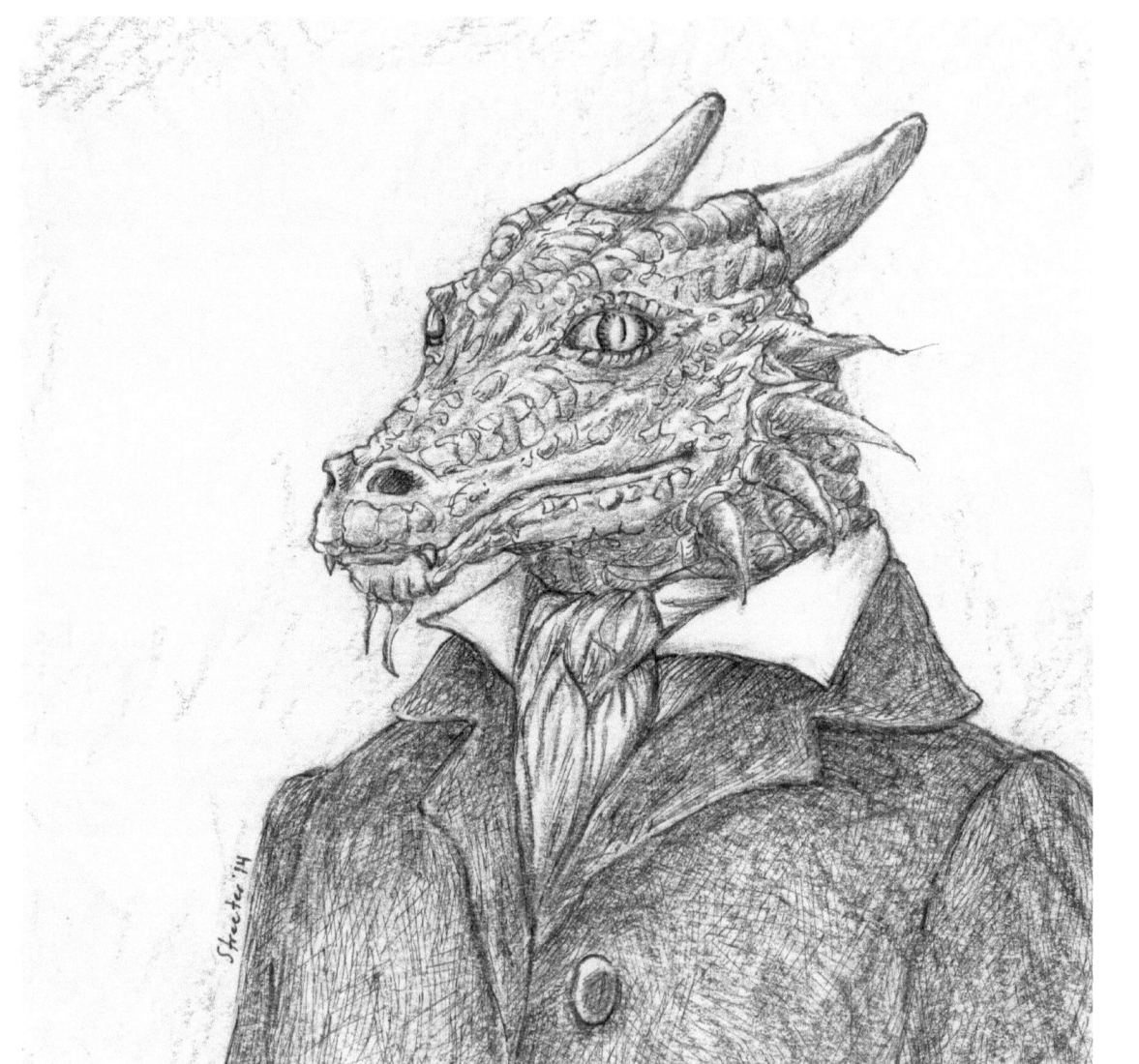

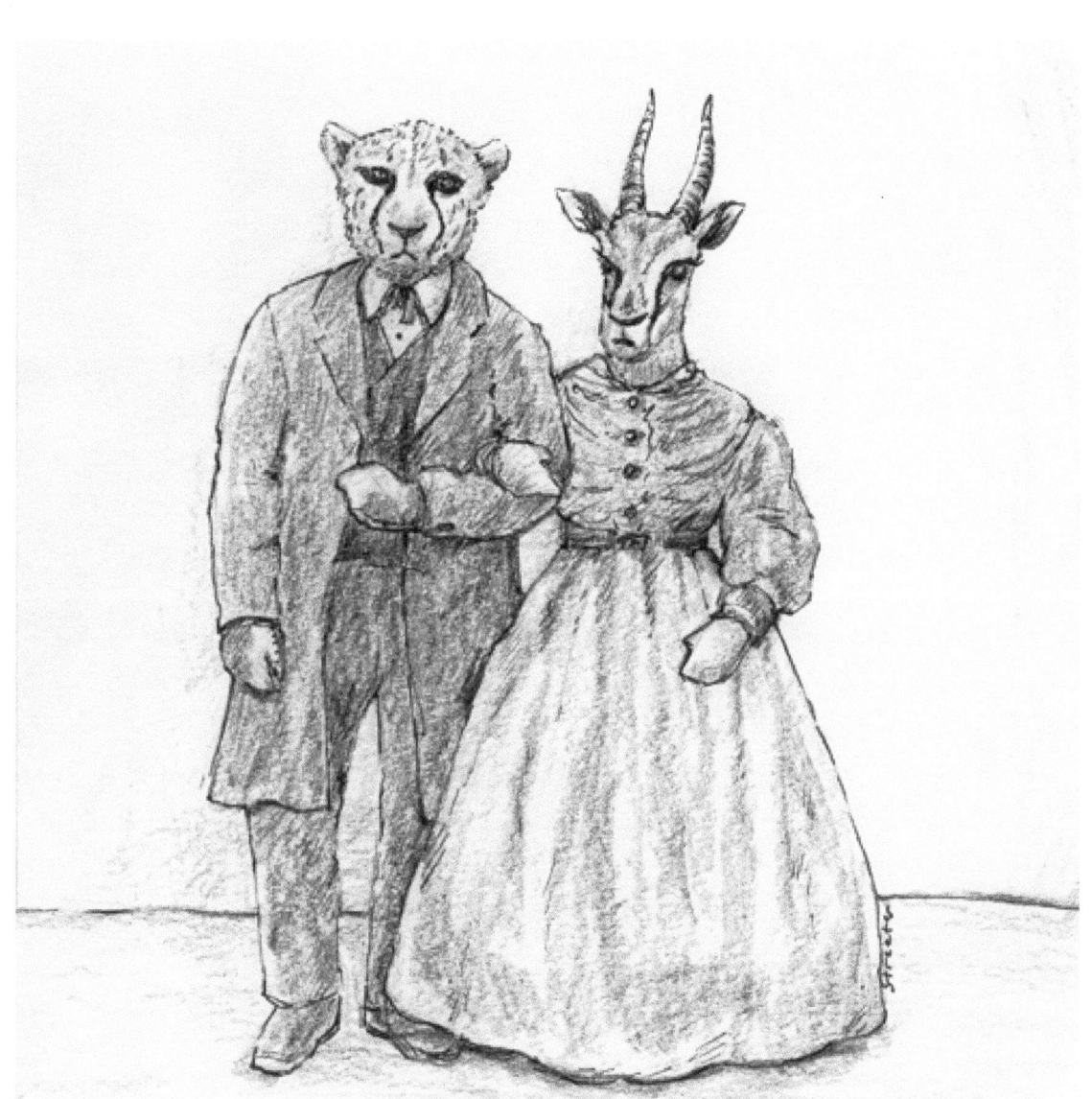

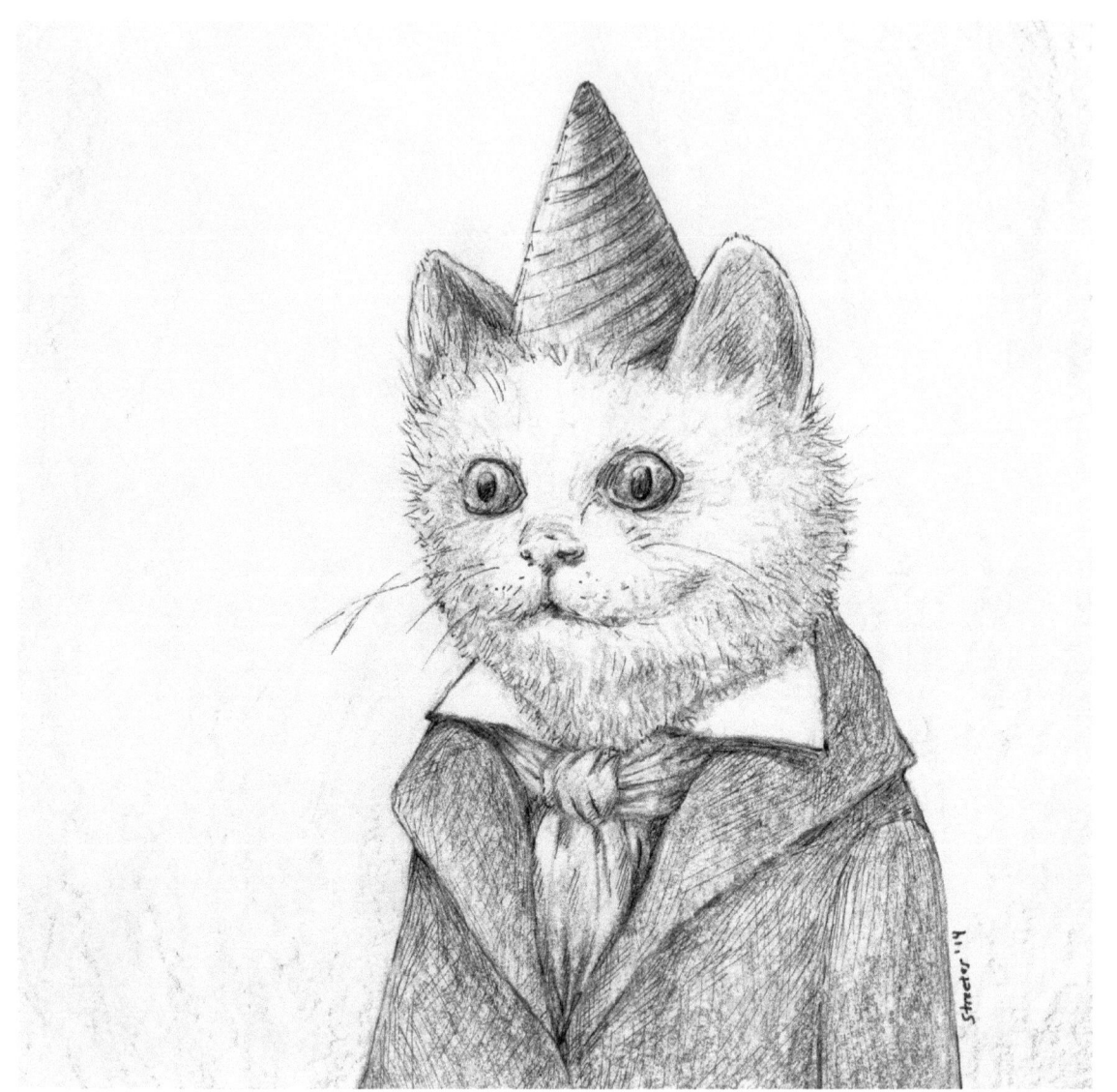

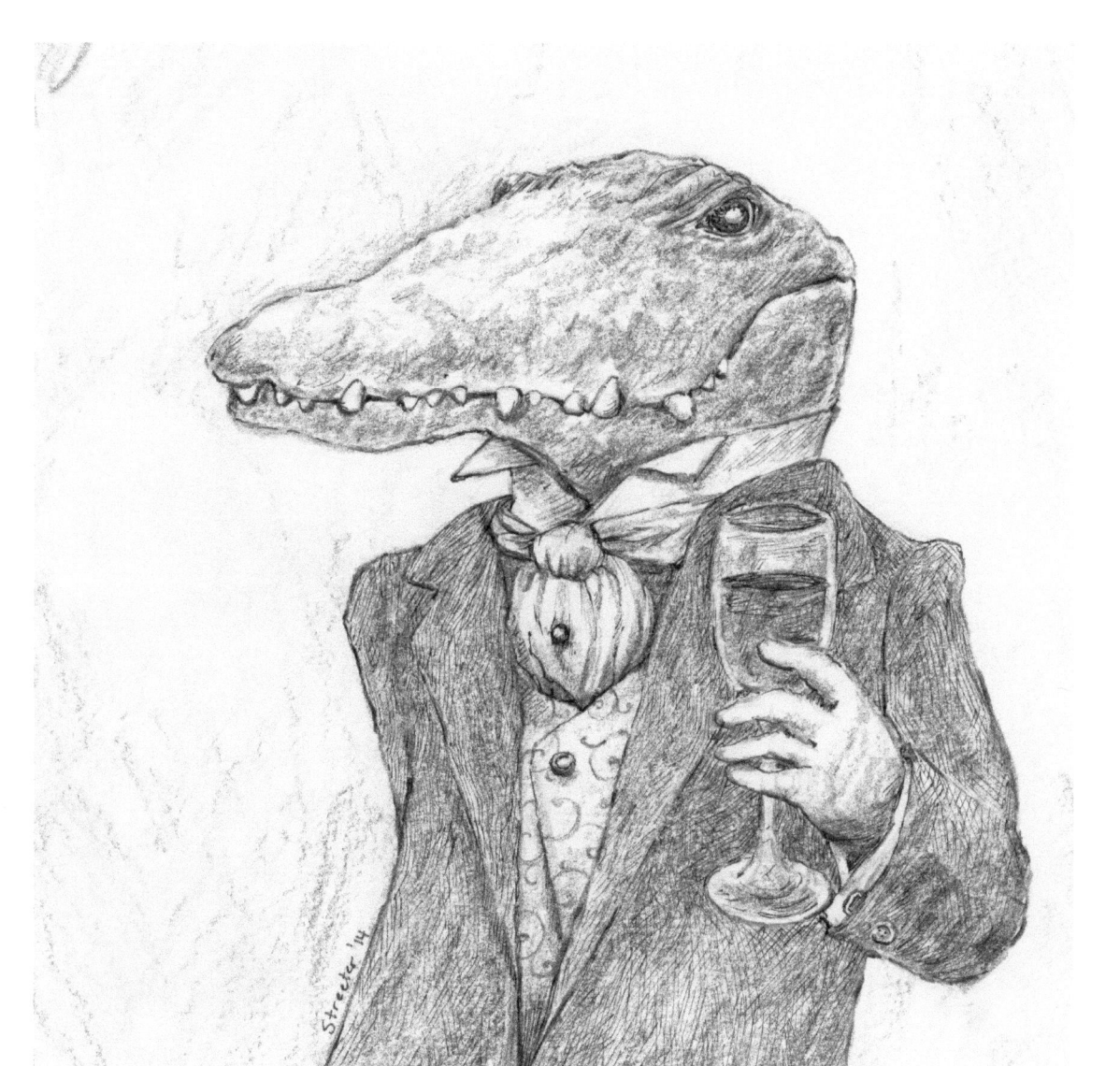

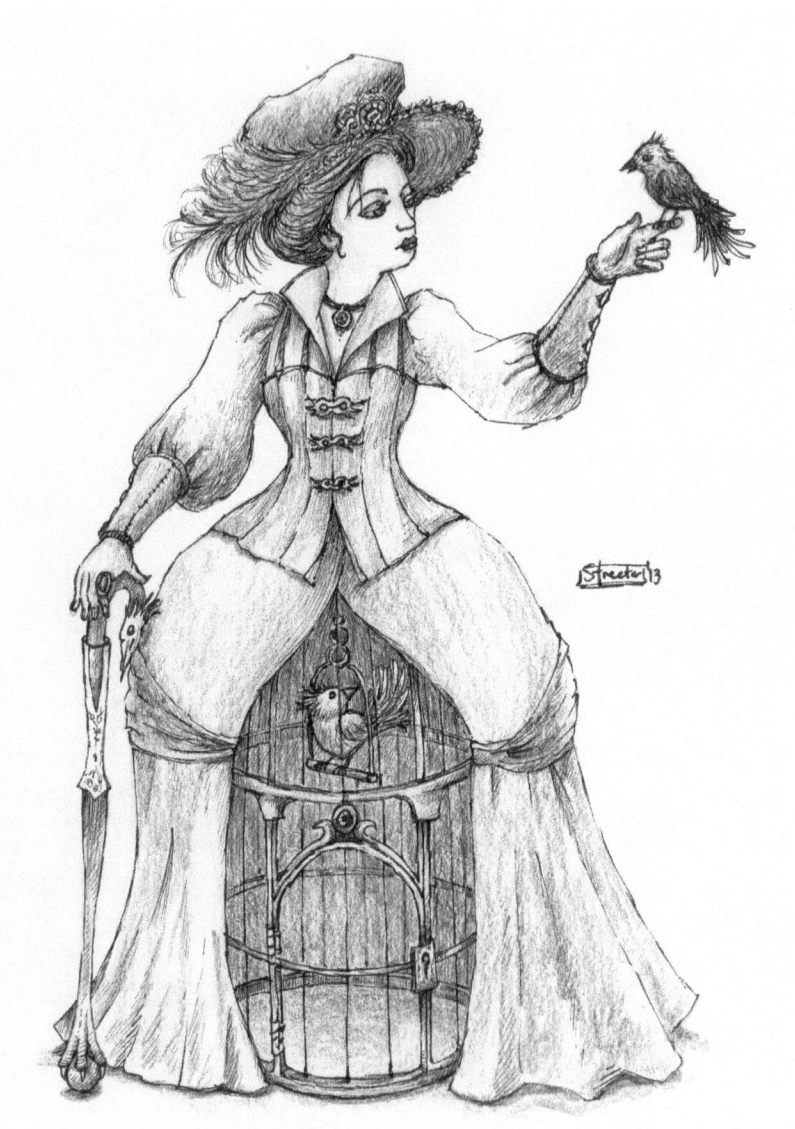

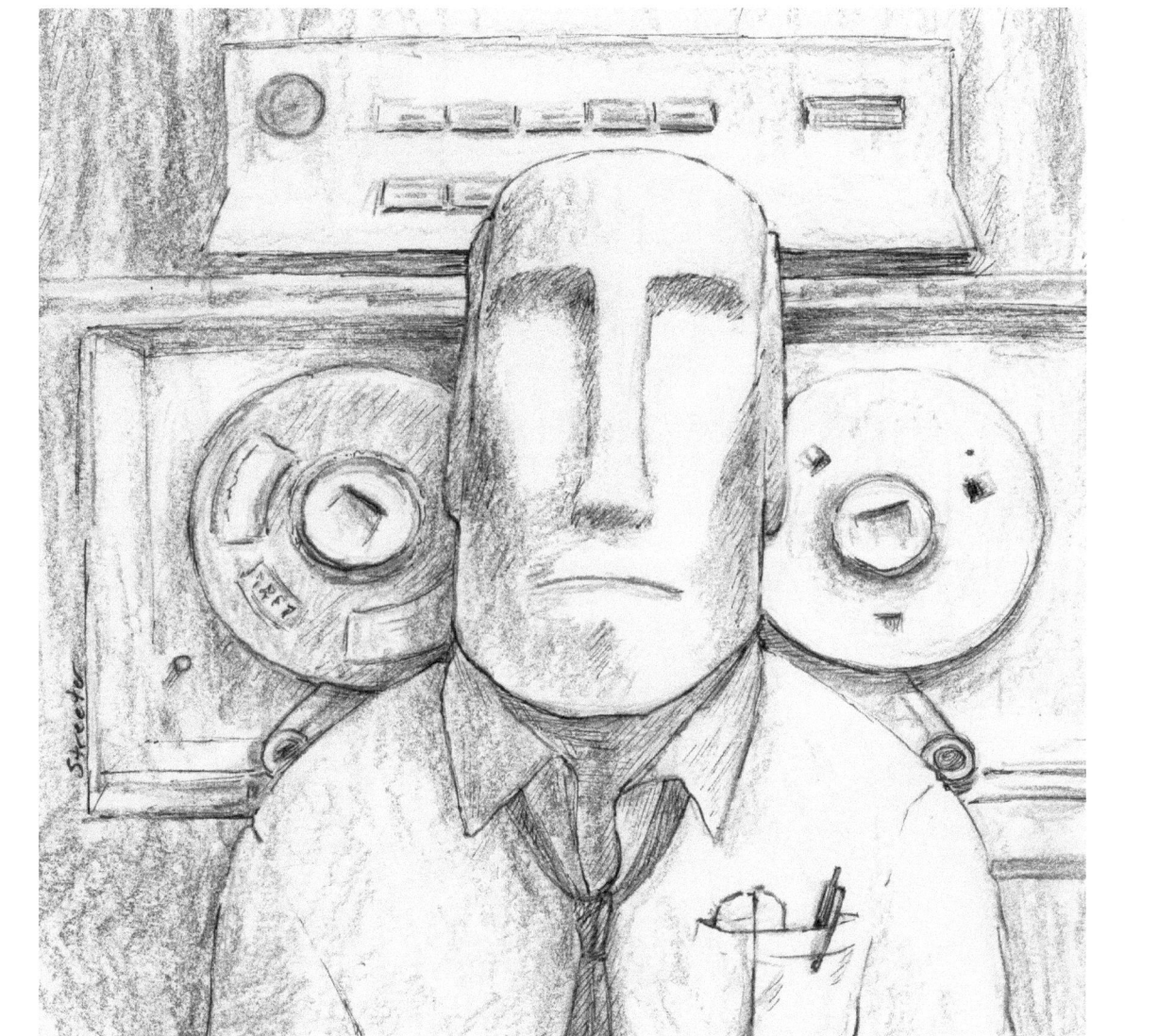

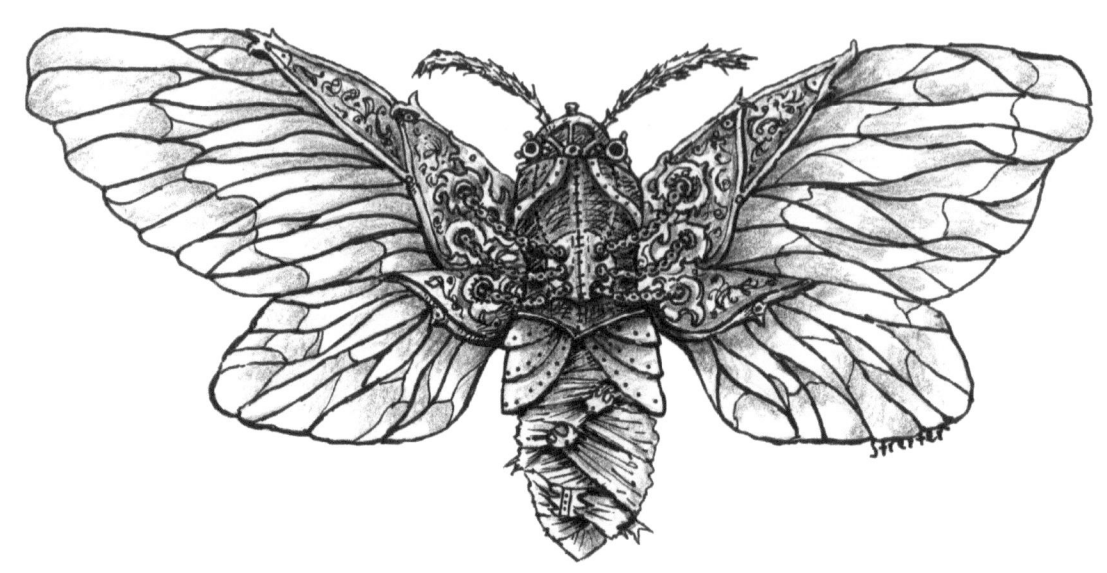

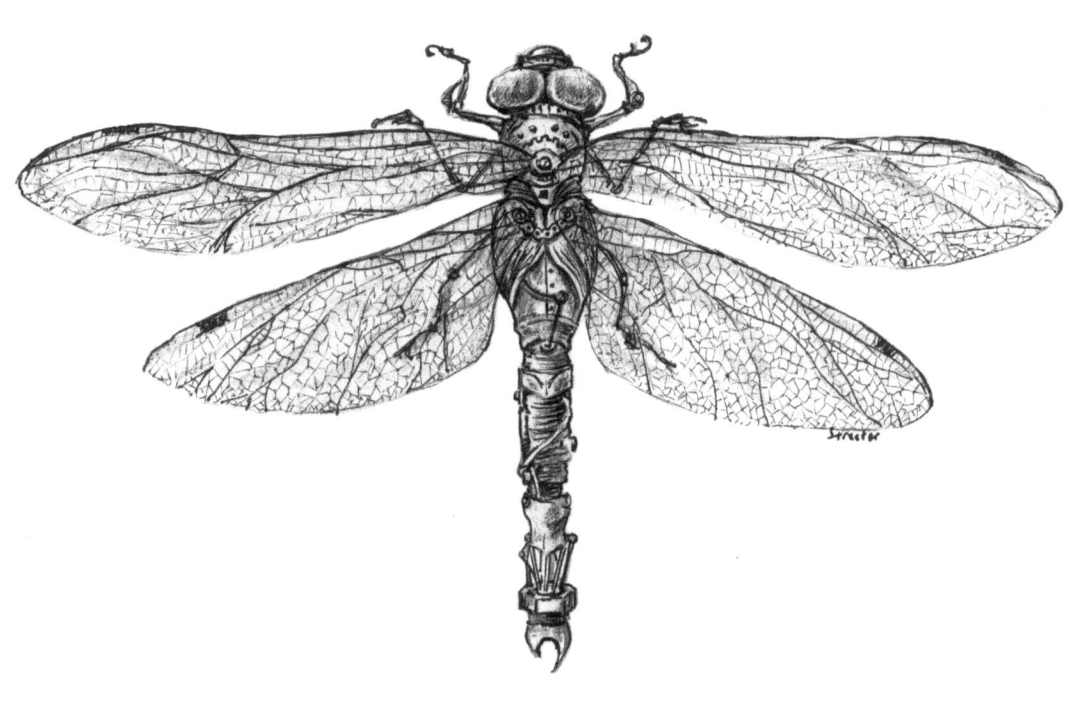

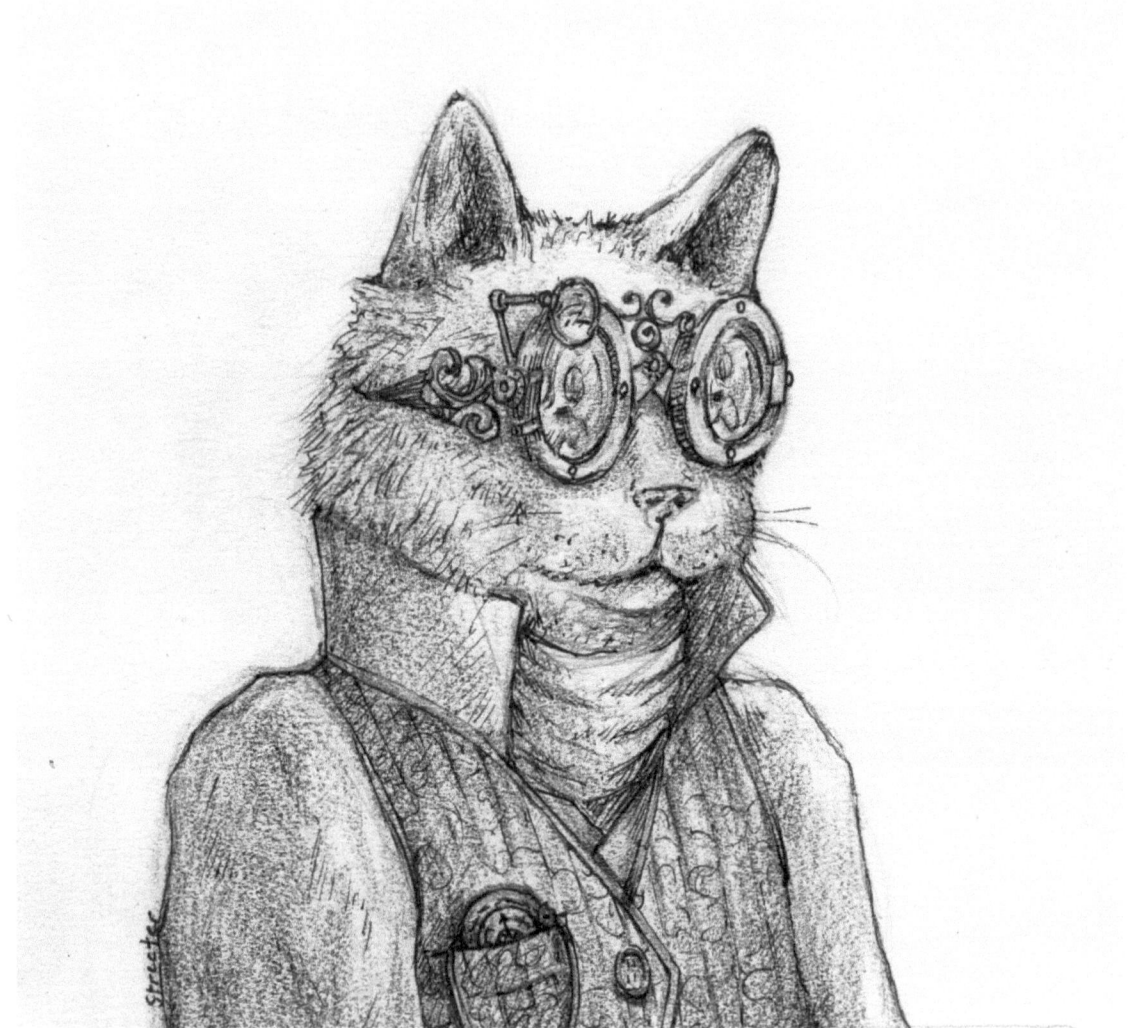

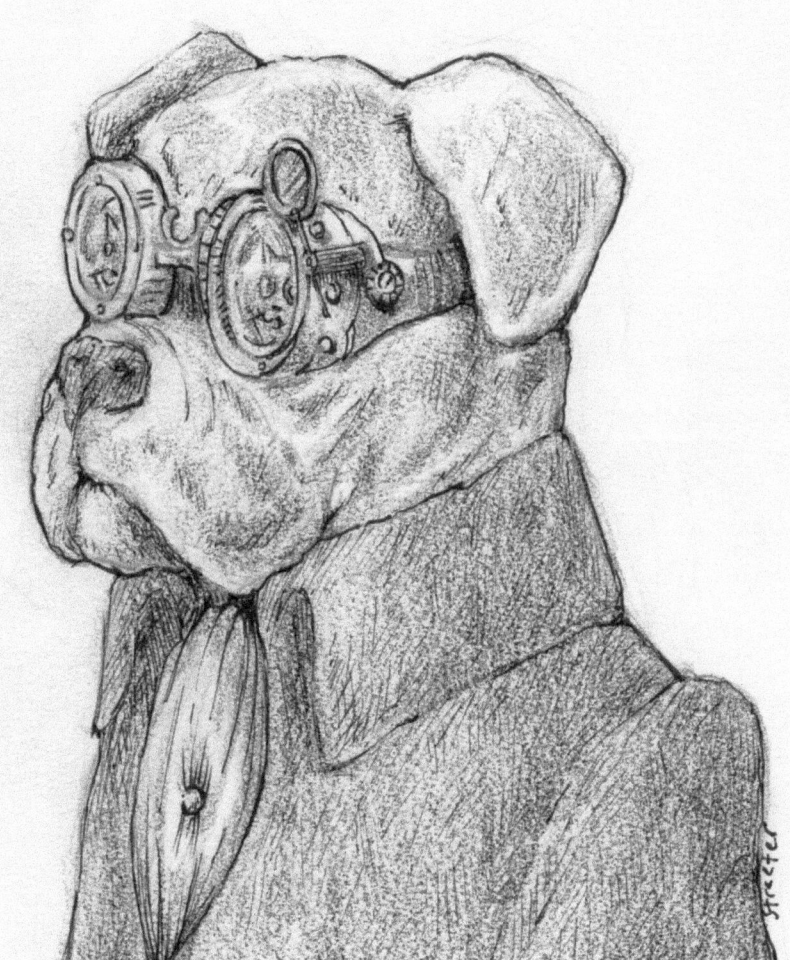

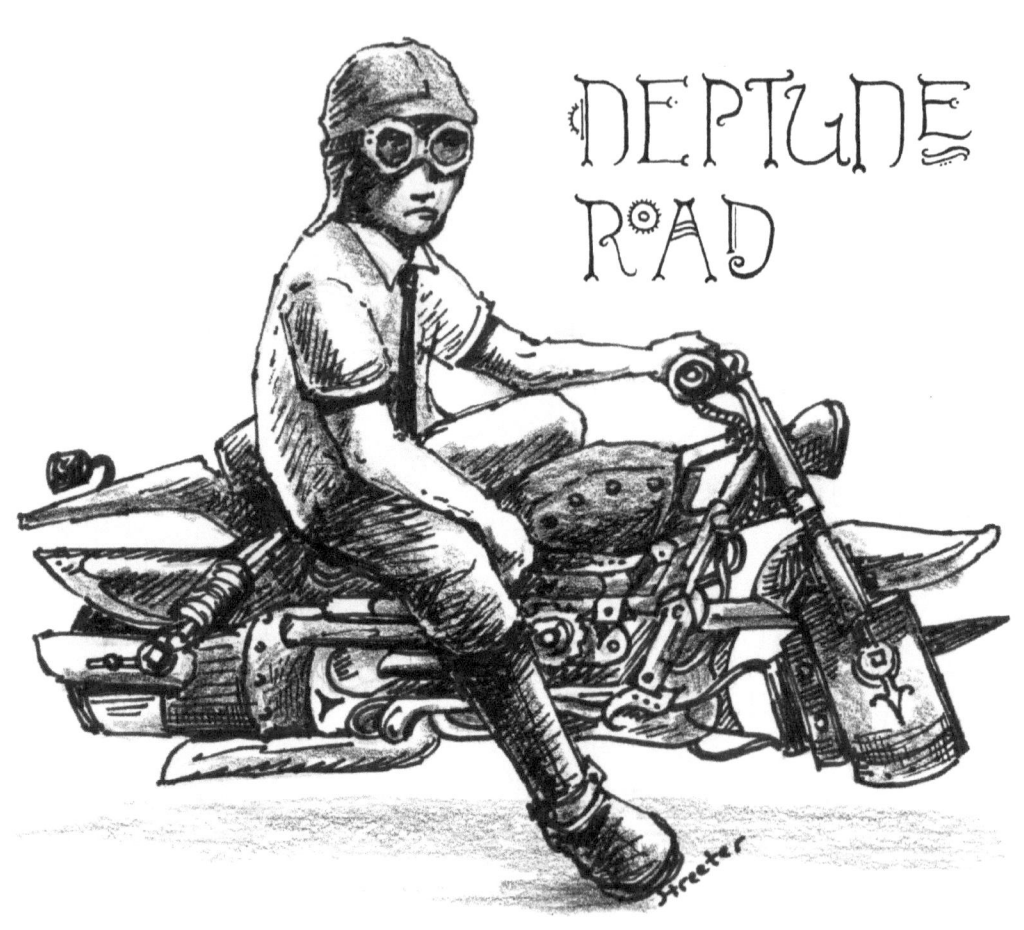

NEPTUNE ROAD

Streeter

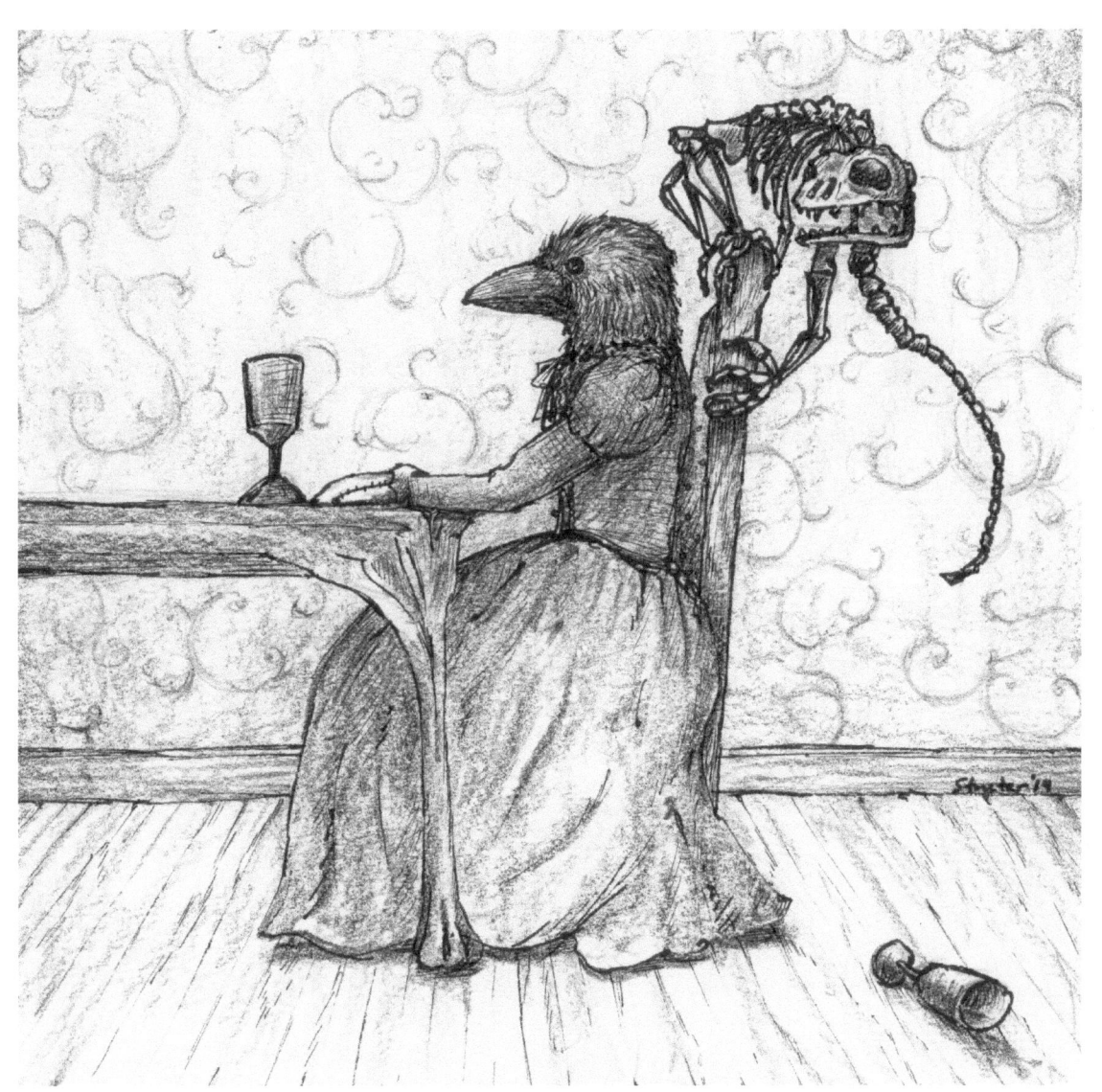

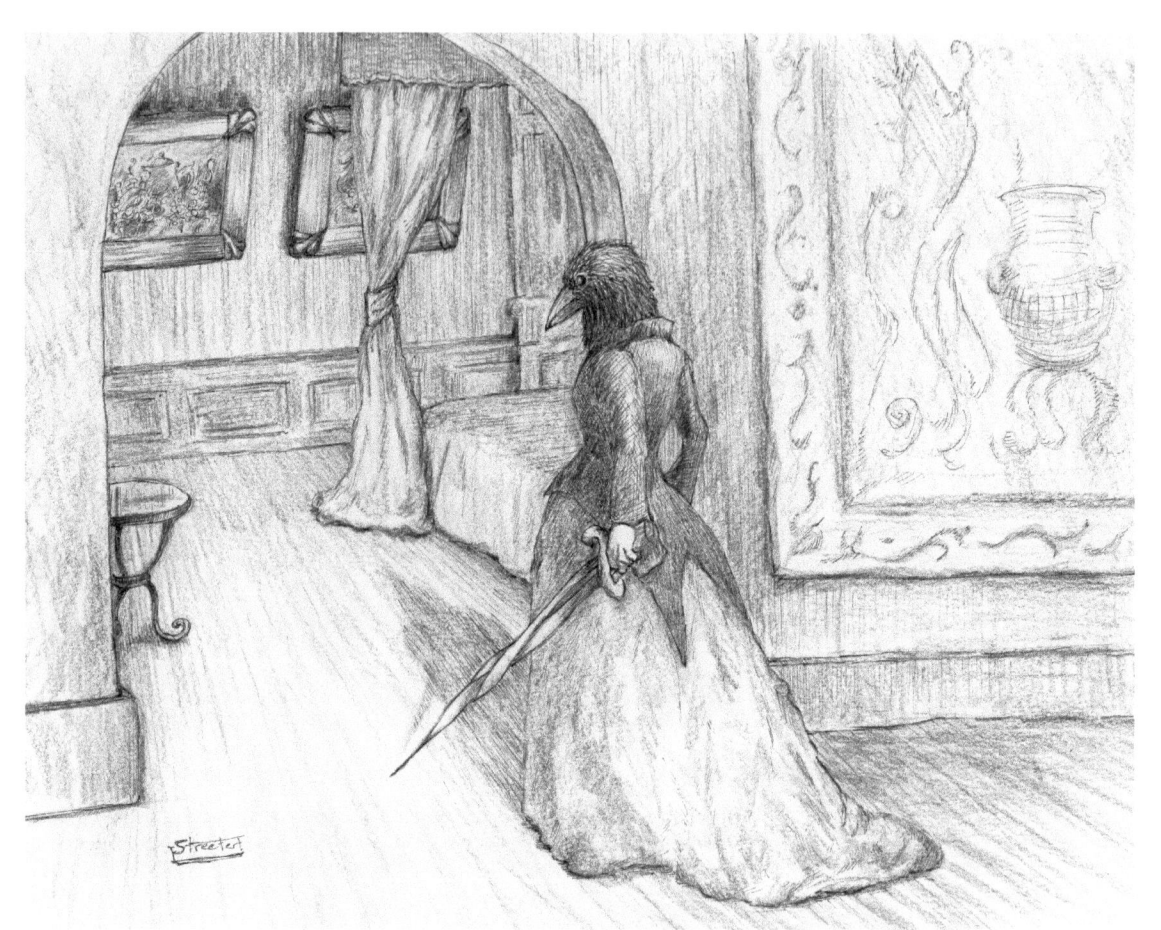

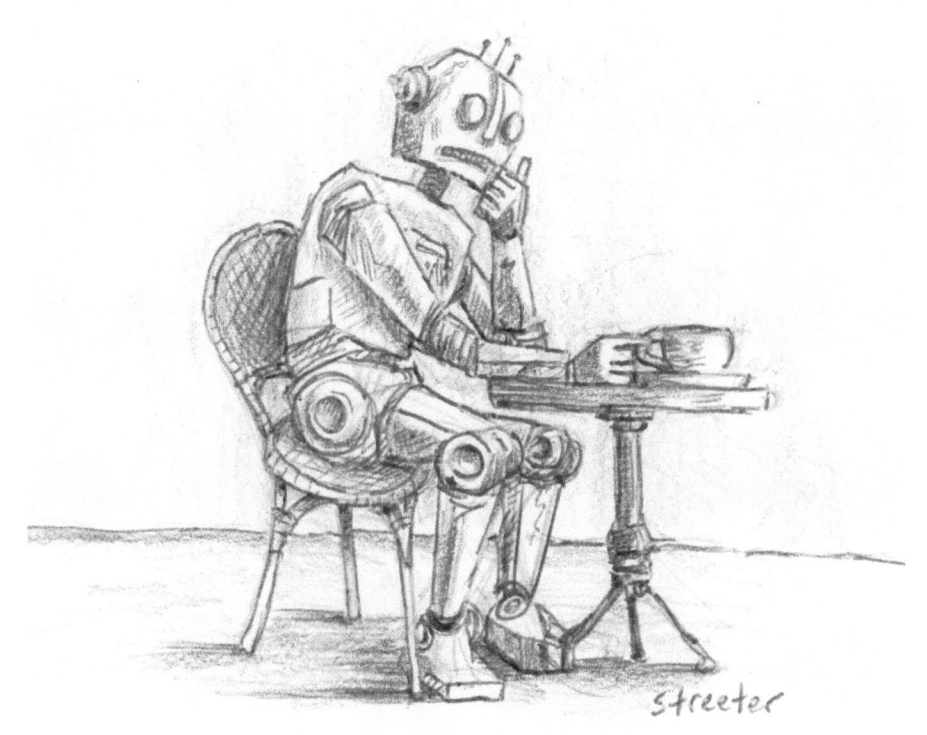

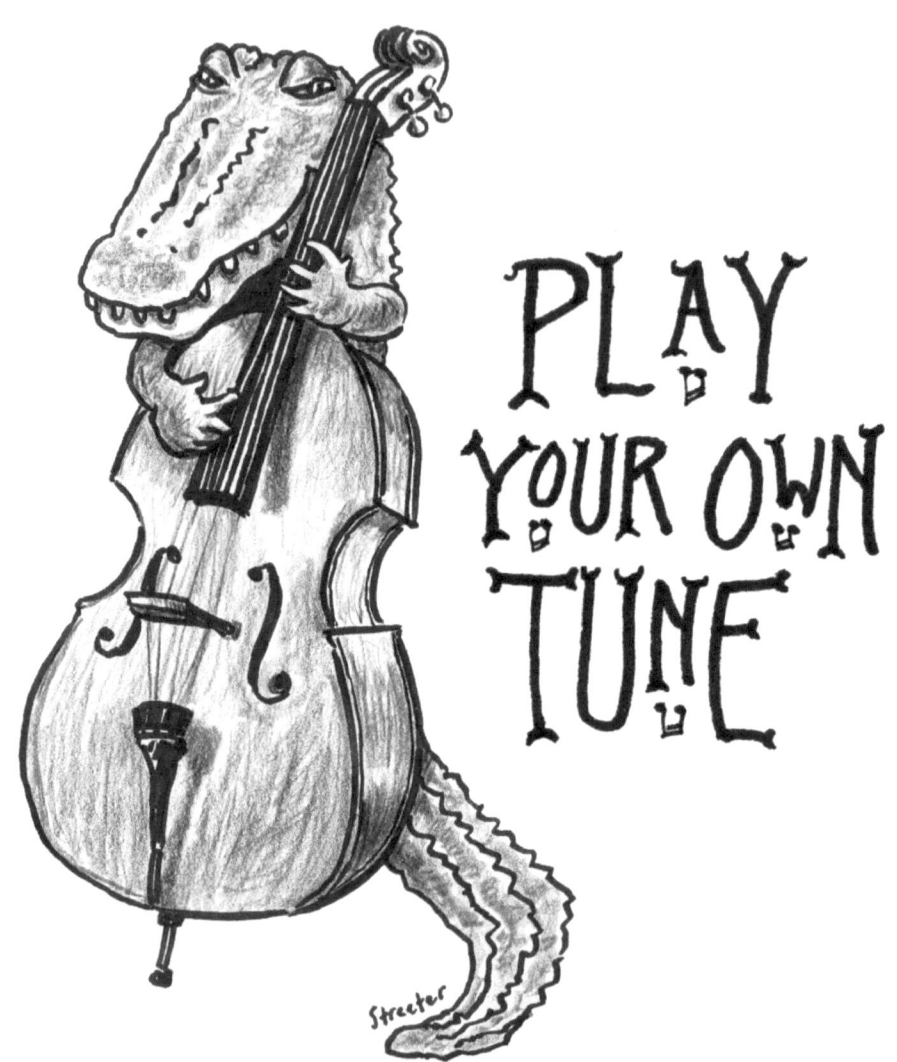

PLAY YOUR OWN TUNE

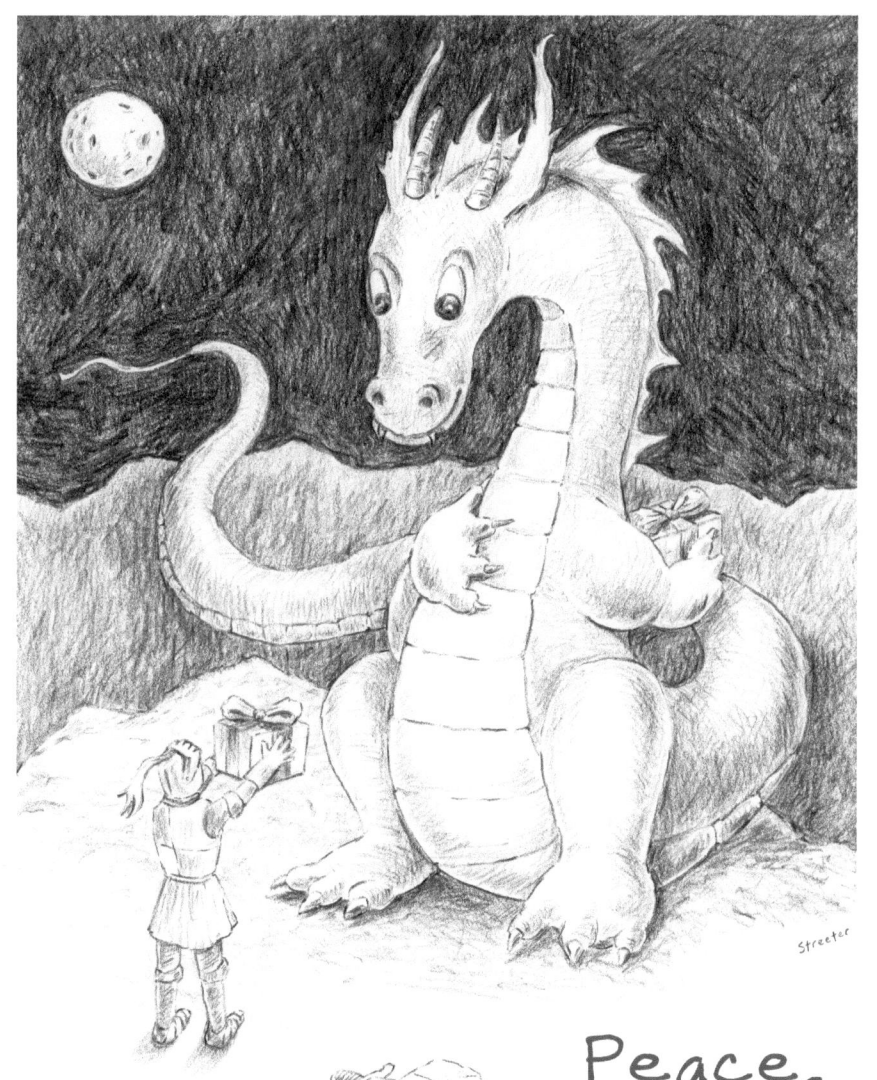

Peace.

About the Artist

Betsy Streeter grew up in a town with a national research laboratory, some cows and a few vineyards. There she learned to program in FORTRAN on a Cray and turned her hair green in the swimming pool. She has driven backwards on a freeway and been paid to make dry ice go through surgical tubing. Her biggest influences growing up were probably David Bowie, Martina Navratilova and Jacques Cousteau. Plus a bunch of other people.

Betsy is the author of a number of books, including the *Silverwood* novels and the illustrated sci fi serial *Neptune Road*. Her single-panel cartoons (originally seen in the feature, *Brainwaves*) and other artwork travel the world in book, magazine, presentation, website, traveling science exhibit and tattoo form.

She is always hatching new projects and artwork and you can keep up with the whole mess at www.betsystreeter.com.

Rocket On!

www.ingramcontent.com/pod-product-compliance
Lightning Source LLC
Chambersburg PA
CBHW050907180526
45159CB00007B/2826